Little People, BIG DREAMS™
ROSALIND FRANKLIN

Written by
Maria Isabel Sánchez Vegara

Illustrated by
Naomi Wilkinson

Frances Lincoln
Children's Books

Little Rosalind was a Jewish girl from London.
She was determined, curious, and eager to learn.

Whenever her family traveled, Rosalind left her dolls at home.
She preferred to play board games with her dad!

She attended St. Paul's, one of the few girls' schools that taught science at the time. Every year, Rosalind was top of the class in all subjects except music. Her teacher wondered if she suffered from a hearing problem.

But Rosalind only had eyes and ears for chemistry—
the science that reveals what everything is made of.

She won a college scholarship that she gladly gave
to another student who needed it more than her.

Rosalind was studying chemistry at Newnham College when she met a girl from Paris called Adrienne. She was one of Marie Curie's students. Over long conversations in French about their experiments, they became friends.

Thanks to a fellowship, Rosalind joined the chemistry lab at the University of Cambridge. But she quickly realized that her boss had no intention of fostering her talent. Instead, she quit her job to study an important material: coal.

When the war started, her discoveries about coal helped
the British Army improve masks and save many lives. Still,
Rosalind wanted to do more! At night, she volunteered,
helping civilians find shelter during air raids.

After the war, and with her friend Adrienne's help, Rosalind got a dream job in Paris. For the next five years, she experimented with X-ray techniques to take pictures of the tiniest substance in chemistry: molecules.

Back home at King's College, her colleagues were
trying to sort out the secrets of DNA: the molecules that
contain all the information our bodies need to grow,
from the size of our toenails to the color of our hair.

Rosalind was asked to take a picture of DNA's structure to see how all this information is stored. She was the only scientist in the world with enough knowledge and experience to succeed in such a thrilling challenge.

It took Rosalind and her assistant Raymond one hundred hours to get Photograph 51. Reviewing the image, they proved that DNA looks like two staircases twisted into a spiral. It was a major moment for science!

But when Rosalind left King's College, some of her colleagues used the photo as evidence for their studies—without giving her credit for it. They later won a Nobel Prize that Rosalind also deserved to share.

It took others a long time to recognize her achievements,
but Rosalind didn't wait. She was already busy studying
the tiny structure of something else: viruses. She worked
to understand them for the rest of her life.

Because little Rosalind, one of the most important chemists of all time, never thought of science as a race. But as an honest process of learning and discovery, and an opportunity to help humankind.

ROSALIND FRANKLIN

(Born 1920 • Died 1958)

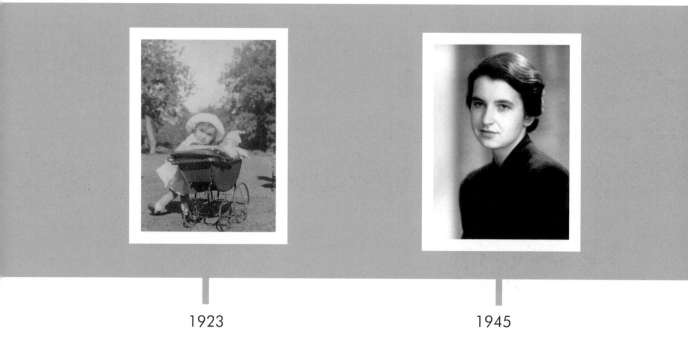

1923   1945

Born in Notting Hill, London, Rosalind Elsie Franklin arrived into the open
arms of an affluent and influential Jewish family on July 25th, 1920.
Rosalind's father Ellis was a partner at a bank and also at the publisher,
Routledge, and he and his wife Muriel gave their time to local charities and
community services. Rosalind started at St. Paul's School for Girls, which
emphasized preparing girls for careers—and not just for marriage. She
demonstrated an early talent for math and science, and was soon fluent
in French, Italian, and German. The Franklin's family vacations were spent
on walking and hiking tours—an activity that became one of Rosalind's
lifelong passions. By the age of 15, Rosalind knew that she wanted to be
a scientist. She enrolled at Newnham College, Cambridge, in 1938 and

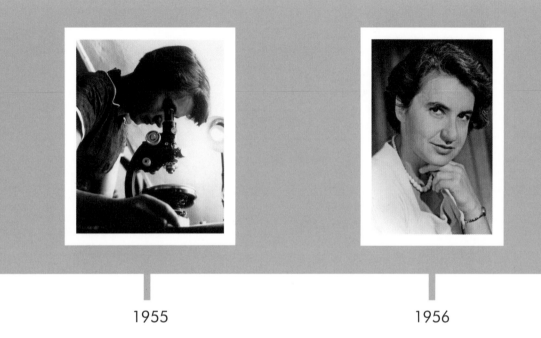

1955

1956

studied chemistry. Three years later, she went on to work as an assistant research officer at the British Coal Utilization Research Association. There, she determined that different types of coal have different microstructures, which predicted their usefulness for different tasks. In 1946, Rosalind's research led her to discover "the secret of life"—the double helix structure of DNA, changing the future of science forever. In doing so, she also pioneered the use of X-rays to create different types of images and analyze unfamiliar matter. She worked up to her death in 1958. Rosalind did not get the recognition her male colleagues shared when they won the 1962 Nobel Prize for this ground-breaking work, but now we consider her as one of the most brilliant scientists of all time.

Want to find out more about **Rosalind Franklin?**

Have a read of these great books:

Unlocking DNA by Megan Borgert-Spaniol

Women in Science by Rachel Ignotofsky

Brimming with creative inspiration, how-to projects, and useful information to enrich your everyday life, Quarto Knows is a favourite destination for those pursuing their interests and passions. Visit our site and dig deeper with our books into your area of interest: Quarto Creates, Quarto Cooks, Quarto Homes, Quarto Lives, Quarto Drives, Quarto Explores, Quarto Gifts, or Quarto Kids.

Text © 2021 Maria Isabel Sánchez Vegara. Illustrations © 2021 Naomi Wilkinson.

Original concept of the series by Maria Isabel Sánchez Vegara, published by Alba Editorial, s.l.u

Little People Big Dreams and Pequeña&Grande are registered trademarks of Alba Editorial, s.l.u. for books, printed publications, e-books and audiobooks. Produced under licence from Alba Editorial, s.l.u.

First Published in the US in 2021 by Frances Lincoln Children's Books, an imprint of The Quarto Group.

The Old Brewery, 6 Blundell Street, London N7 9BH, United Kingdom.

T 020 7700 6700 **www.QuartoKnows.com**

A catalogue record for this book is available from the British Library.

ISBN 978-0-7112-5957-7

Set in Futura BT.

Published by Katie Cotton • Designed by Karissa Santos
Edited by Katy Flint • Production by Nikki Ingram
Editorial Assistance from Alex Hithersay
Manufactured In China CC052021
1 3 5 7 9 8 6 4 2

Photographic acknowledgements (pages 28-29, from left to right): 1. Rosalind Franklin at age 3, from the personal collection of Jennifer Glynn, via US National Library of Medicine. 2. Rosalind Franklin (1920-1958), English chemist and DNA pioneer, ca. 1945 © Pictorial Press Ltd / Alamy Stock Photo 3. Rosalind Elsie Franklin (1920-1958) was a British chemist and crystallographer who is best known for her role in the discovery of the structure of DNA. 1955 © Universal History Archive/Universal Images Group via Getty Images 4. 1956 © Universal History Archive/Universal Images Group via Getty Images

MIX
Paper from
responsible sources
FSC® C008047
FSC
www.fsc.org

Collect the *Little People, BIG DREAMS*™ series:

FRIDA KAHLO	COCO CHANEL	MAYA ANGELOU	AMELIA EARHART	AGATHA CHRISTIE	MARIE CURIE	ROSA PARKS

AUDREY HEPBURN	EMMELINE PANKHURST	ELLA FITZGERALD	ADA LOVELACE	JANE AUSTEN	GEORGIA O'KEEFFE	HARRIET TUBMAN

ANNE FRANK	MOTHER TERESA	JOSEPHINE BAKER	L. M. MONTGOMERY	JANE GOODALL	SIMONE DE BEAUVOIR	MUHAMMAD ALI

STEPHEN HAWKING	MARIA MONTESSORI	VIVIENNE WESTWOOD	MAHATMA GANDHI	DAVID BOWIE	WILMA RUDOLPH	DOLLY PARTON

BRUCE LEE	RUDOLF NUREYEV	ZAHA HADID	MARY SHELLEY	MARTIN LUTHER KING JR.	DAVID ATTENBOROUGH	ASTRID LINDGREN

EVONNE GOOLAGONG	BOB DYLAN	ALAN TURING	BILLIE JEAN KING	GRETA THUNBERG	JESSE OWENS	JEAN-MICHEL BASQUIAT

ARETHA FRANKLIN

CORAZON AQUINO

PELÉ

ERNEST SHACKLETON

STEVE JOBS

AYRTON SENNA

LOUISE BOURGEOIS

ELTON JOHN

JOHN LENNON

PRINCE

CHARLES DARWIN

CAPTAIN TOM MOORE

HANS CHRISTIAN ANDERSEN

STEVIE WONDER

MEGAN RAPINOE

MARY ANNING

MALALA YOUSAFZAI

ANDY WARHOL

RUPAUL

MICHELLE OBAMA

MINDY KALING

IRIS APFEL

ROSALIND FRANKLIN

ACTIVITY BOOKS

STICKER ACTIVITY BOOK

COLORING BOOK

LITTLE ME, BIG DREAMS JOURNAL

Discover more about the series at www.littlepeoplebigdreams.com